As a widow of almost 18 months, I very much appreciated having this book to read. Although every circumstance is unique, there seems to be a great deal of similarities as to the grief process. This author nailed so many feelings, that I have had, and others that were completely opposite of my experience. One thing for certain, no one is truly ever ready to let go of their lifelong partner.

In this instance the husband was found very unexpectedly, deceased upon the author coming home. I can hardly imagine what that must be like. I was given the news that my husband had anywhere from 30 days to a year to live. He lived for 13 months. I retired early to spend his last time on earth with him. I KNEW he was dying, and yet, when he did, I was still in a state of shock. When people heard that he had passed, I kept hearing, " Well, you knew this was coming" Yes, I guess I did; we are all closer to our deaths one day at a time. That certainly doesn't mean I was ready. Not for the sights we had shared, not to hear our favorite songs, not to hold onto his pillow and try to smell his special smell not to sit alone in the church pew every Sunday, not to go to small group ALONE, not to be hit with the mountain of paperwork that one's spouse's death creates, not to eat alone, not to try to comfort his family when I couldn't even comfort his beloved dog. I was sure that I couldn't stay in our home and have to come home every night to him not being here. But, he Wanted me to Stay here! How can I not do what he wanted?

Time doesn't heal us, but it does change our perception of things. *And Then There Was One* was a great help to me. It helped me know that the feelings I have are not good or bad, but Normal. I highly recommend this book, especially to those who are early in their grief. I wish I had had it sooner!

— **Christina Duncan, widow**

And Then There Was One

An Emotionally Raw
Journey through
Spousal Grief

MARY ECHOLS

Deep River
B O O K S

And Then There Was One: An Emotionally Raw Journey through Spousal Grief
© 2019 by Mary Echols

Published by Deep River Books
Sisters, Oregon
www.deepriverbooks.com

Printed in the United States of America

Scripture verses quoted are from the King James Version. Public domain.

ISBN – 13: 9781632695024
Library of Congress: 2019908267

Printed in the USA
2019—First Edition

28 27 26 25 24 23 22 21   10 9 8 7 6 5 4 3 2

Cover Design by Robin Black, Inspirio Design

Dedication

To Lynn Stoeckel, my dear friend, who heard a voice she felt needed to be shared.

Contents

Introduction

What you are holding in your hand is my journal—a description of my journey through grieving the death of my husband. Keep in mind as you read this that it is my journey, not yours. There are things in this journey of mine that will mirror the struggles you are going through, and there are things that you will deal with that I didn't. Each of us has to pave our own way and the way will, at times, make you question so much. But understand that no matter how strange your journey may seem, all your topsy-turvy emotions are normal. Our journeys are molded by age, culture, religion (or lack of such), life experiences, support systems, and a myriad of other things. We all must walk through grief to healing, and we will all do it in our own way and at our own pace.

There is no time limit to grieving but that doesn't give you license to wallow in it forever, either. At some time, you must make the decision to step away from grief and begin to have a life again. This can be frightening because the problem is not having a new life but doing it alone.

As an RN, I have been at so many bedsides of patients who were dying, then died; and have sat with so many family members who were beginning the grieving process. I understood about death and dying. At least I thought I did. I had information from nursing school; I had been to seminars and listened to educated speakers who told the clinical aspects of grief. I felt prepared for this part of life that I saw on, sometimes, a daily basis.

However, the clinical side of grieving in no way prepares you for going through the actual journey of grief. Knowing about grieving from what I learned in books and seminars was of little help when I actually had to walk through it myself. Knowing about the five steps of grieving let me know that denial, anger, bargaining, depression, and acceptance were normal. I knew that these were guideposts but not written in stone. It wasn't the steps that were the problem. The problem was they were just an outline, and I wanted and needed more than an outline.

After my husband died, I began looking for something I could read that would allow me into someone else's journey and help me to see that the little things I was stressing over were okay. I needed to know that someone else couldn't change the sheets, that someone else washed her spouse's clothes with hers, that someone else would open his bathroom drawer that held hairbrush, aftershave, cologne, and breathe in his scent. I needed to have these things validated!

Because there was nothing written I could find, I began to journal. I began to write all these "strange" behaviors down and I found that seeing these things in print began to help me deal with them. Not only did journaling help with emotions but it gave me a way to look back over time and see how far I had come in my grieving. It also gave me the ability to see where my stumbling blocks to moving on were. Journaling allowed me to see how I was growing and maturing through this process of grief.

You are reading this because a precious friend kept telling me that what I had journaled was what I looked for and couldn't find. Her gentle persistence over the years has brought this to you and my prayer is you will find the validation for what you are going through that I couldn't.

My prayer is that as you read this journal and answer the questions, you will begin to see your way through your grief. My walk was strengthened by my favorite book of the Bible, the book of Psalms, and one particular verse I leaned on that sustained me, Psalms 30:11: "Thou hast turned for me my mourning into dancing: thou hast put off my sackcloth and girded me with gladness" (KJV). My prayer for you is that one day soon you will know Psalm 30:11.

And Then There Was One . . .

Did you ever stop and consider how one seemingly simple act can change your world—bumping into a stranger who turns out to be your best friend for life, helping someone who turns out to be your new boss, or turning a doorknob and stepping into a world you didn't want, didn't ask for, and didn't know how to navigate?

That was me. I simply opened the door.

I opened the front door and, as I looked down the entry hall into the living room, I saw you sitting in your recliner. The angle of the chair put its back to me, and I was immediately struck by the fact that you didn't call out to me as you usually did. Also, there was something about the position of your head that made my heart drop as my stomach rose to catch it. I called to you and was met with dread silence. Somehow, I found myself at the front of your chair, looking at you. My breath stopped, and my heart spiraled, as I looked at the face of death before me.

As a seasoned RN, I had occasionally wondered how I would react in this kind of situation, and if all the years of training would detach me long enough to do what needed to be done or if I would fall apart and become helpless. The training paid off as I reached to check for a pulse and pupil response, in what seemed like simultaneous actions, dialed 9-1-1—and then my neighbor, to help me—as I started CPR for what I knew was a futile effort.

The ambulance finally arrived, along with the sheriff's department. After time of death was pronounced, I was given a few minutes alone to say goodbye, and you were gone. And there I sat on the floor, having opened the door of our home a wife and stepped into it a widow. Dead . . . you *and* me.

One normal, ordinary, casual act of opening a door—nothing more—and my life was forever changed. In one fell swoop, I went from wife to widow, married to single, together to alone.

I watched as my husband was taken away, a robot who mechanically closed the door, then turned and went to the phone to call our children and tell them their father was dead. The news was met with the sounds of sucked-in breath and silence. And then the questions began, and the tears started to fall. Each call was harder than the one before, because with each call my reality began to set in.

⁓ ⌒ ⁓

Sudden death is horrible. Sudden death leaves such a host of things undone. I walked in our home and there you were . . . dead. There was no time to ask questions or get answers about anything, no time to say goodbye, no time for a last hug and kiss, no time to say . . . I love you.

⁓ ⌒ ⁓

It's the end of the first day without you. The children have arrived, and the embracing and tears of our loss and the hushed, heartbroken conversation is over. Exhaustion has taken its toll on everyone, so sleeping arrangements are made and bedroom doors are quietly closing—all the bedroom doors but mine. I stand in the living room staring down the hall toward our room. Our room—it's always been our room until today, and now there is no longer an "our," just mine.

With flowing tears and spaghetti legs I start down the hall. All I can think about is that twenty-four hours ago, we were walking down this hall together. If only I had known it would be the last time, I would have committed every word to memory. I would have taken you by the hand and led you to our bed; we would have made love all night and "I love you" would have pealed out like church bells on Sunday morning. But I didn't know.

I enter our room. It's so quiet, so deathly quiet. There's no sound of you showering, brushing your teeth, or the mundane chatter about nothing that fills the air before we go to bed. We . . . there's no we . . . and I have to face that bed alone, just me, by myself. I stumble into the closet in search of something to sleep in, but I don't want to go to sleep and I certainly don't want to get into that bed alone. My heart is thumping so hard that I think it will burst out of my chest. The wellspring of tears that haven't stopped all day are gushing once more, and with them come the gut-wrenching sobs I try so hard to stifle so that I won't awaken anyone. All I want is you, but you're not here. I reach in the closet and pull out one of your shirts, and with palsied fingers attempt the buttons and begin the journey to the bed.

⌒ ℭ ℈ ⌒

Memories, memories flood my mind. I lie on my back and feel the river of tears running down the sides of my head, into my hair, and soaking the pillow. I reach my hand to where your body should be, and I feel nothing but the cold, unwelcoming sheets where last night there had been warm, welcoming arms that cuddled me in and held me close to you, while the cool sheets warmed around us and I drifted off to sleep in the safety of those arms.

I turn my head toward your side of the bed. I reach for your pillow, and as I bring it to me the scent of you floods my senses and I am defeated. The racking sobs come in wave after wave and I'm buried in my grief. At some point my mind finally says, "No more," and at last I sleep.

I have no idea how I got through that first night. I assume I went to sleep because of the lapse of unaccounted-for time from my memory. I would have been content to not have awakened but there was no choice and I now had to get up and face what was to come.

You died yesterday and today I'm picking out your casket. I don't want to do this. Our children are here helping me to walk through the motions and to answer questions I don't want to answer . . . obituary questions, cause-of-death questions, cemetery questions, questions, questions, questions until I could scream! You should be here answering all these questions about you—why aren't you? Why did you leave me to do this alone, to *be* alone? Tomorrow is "the visitation." Why do they call it that when you aren't visiting anyone, and I don't want to?

Reality hits hard when you're answering questions, picking out a casket, and making plans to have the funeral in another state. The reality that there is no one to help with decisions, that you're on your own, and that this is the way it may always be is a bitter pill to swallow.

~~~~

Later that day, the funeral home called to let me know they had finished with the preparations—which is a nice way of saying that they had finished with *you*—and that, if the family would like we could come by this evening, before they leave with you in the morning on the trip back home for the funeral. I'm not ready for this, but I go.

We are met at the door of the funeral home and ushered into the room where you are. My breath catches in my throat as I look at the reality of your death. I ask everyone to leave me and shut the door behind them.

I am here standing over your casket looking at you, and I swear you look like you could open your eyes any minute and laugh at my grief . . . oh, please do; take this from me. I love you so. How am I going to go on without you? Don't you know I'm kissing you . . . so cold . . . why are you so cold? Why am I so cold? *Oh, dear God, take this from me. I'm not ready.*

The mortician did a wonderful job with my husband's body. When I looked in the casket, I would have sworn it was all a joke and that he was going to open his eyes and laugh at me. He looked so alive, but he felt so dead, cold, hard, and dead. I remember that whole moment as if it were yesterday, and I remember every tiny emotion that was within me to the last detail. I remember my breath being sucked out of my body and my eyes welling up with tears, the chill that came over me, and the way I grabbed hold of the casket to steady myself—only to feel it start to tip under my weight. I remember thinking my heart was going to stop and I remember I was so angry when it didn't. I remember pulling myself together and walking to the door to allow the children in with me. I didn't really want to open the door; I wanted so much more time alone with him, but I knew my time was limited. I remember walking out of the funeral home feeling just as dead as he was.

The next day was a blur as we tried to get everyone ready for the trip. I had no idea what to put on or take, and packing was insane. However, having something to focus on kept the tears at bay, for a time, and allowed a modicum of organization to get the trip started. It was during the packing of suitcases that something happened—something that began my understanding of God's place in this event and the knowledge that He was there with me.

We looked everywhere for my daughter-in-law's shoes. In the closet, under the chest, under the bed, in everyone's luggage, in the living room under all the furniture, the bathroom, dining room, and lastly, the car, although I don't know why because she took them off before she went to bed. We looked everywhere but couldn't find them, and since we were in a hurry to leave, to follow the hearse taking your body back home to bury you, we started off to the cars. As I hit the bottom step, I remembered something and went back in the house, down the hall to our bedroom, then back down the hall past the room they had slept in. I don't know why, but something caught my eye. I stopped, dumbfounded, not believing what I was seeing, but there in the middle of the room—where we had all been walking moments before—were her shoes, just sitting there. And I knew, and I thanked God for allowing us this very precious moment alone to say goodbye. I felt your presence so profoundly, and I knew you wanted me to know you were there. I told you I loved you and not to worry because I'd be okay. After all, God promised to take over the caring for me that you had done. And with that, I blew a kiss toward heaven, and left the house with shoes in hand.

Wow. If there was ever a moment, that was it. No shoes . . . shoes. No explanation but the hand of God—the comforting, ever-present hand of almighty God reaching out to me in my pain and distress. I will always thank Him for that moment alone with you to say goodbye.

⌒ᙅᵗ ᙆᵓ⌒

Now for the four-hour trip, which was all the time I had to plan what I wanted for the funeral. I'm not sure how I put it together. I do know that I buried myself in the Psalms in order to come up with what I wanted said.

I look out the window as the car goes down the road—the road we last went down together to visit your family. I find it hard to see as my eyes are raining tears that have no intention of stopping, and my mind keeps reminding me this will be our last trip together. Even though you're not in the car with me, I know you're on the same road at the same time, so in a way it is "our" last trip. I know that the next time I make this trip I will be alone. I bury myself in my Bible as I pick out verses for the funeral.

I don't remember much about the trip except the tears and the struggle to read Bible verses through those tears. My mind wasn't working properly, so choosing what I wanted said was difficult. I knew you would want the service to be simple—and yet, for me, there needed to be a message that would show God's love and compassion, one that would get all of us mourners through this grief. As usual, when I'm at a loss for words, or a way to express my feelings, I go to the book of Psalms and I am always met with a plethora of ways that I can reach out to God. I could spend a lifetime in Psalms and never get my fill.

I also found, as I explored the book of Psalms for just what I wanted to say, that the Lord was opening up to me the beginning of my healing. I knew from the first moment that He was carrying me, but it was at this moment I actually took the first tenuous baby step toward healing.

❦

It's peculiar how the mind can pick and choose what it wants to remember. I don't remember much about arriving at our destination, but I do remember picking out a tombstone and what should be on it. I also remember sitting down with my daughter-in-law and finding we had picked some of the same Bible verses. I remember being with my husband's brother and sister-in-law and talking about plans, but that's about all I remember until the actual time of the funeral.

❦

Ashes to ashes, dust to dust. Is someone saying that? Where am I? Oh yes, the gravesite under the tent. I'm under the tent, surrounded by our children. Our children—or are they now my children? No, they will always be our children. Listening, watching, silent tears dripping onto shaking hands, other hands reaching to me, words of intended consolation all around me, but my ears refuse to hear them. Go? What? Go and leave you here alone in that box in the ground? Go and leave you without me? Go and leave me without you? Are you people crazy? What? Yes, of course, I have to go.

Walking away from the gravesite was so very hard. I knew I had to, but my feet didn't want to move. Probably what made it so hard was the fact I would now have to make the four-hour journey home. From now on, I wouldn't be able to just get up in the morning and go to the cemetery. On the other hand, that may have been a good thing, for I'm quite sure that's exactly where I would have spent my time for the first several weeks—and if I had done that, it would have kept me from starting down the road to healing.

Since I was so far away, I had no choice but to begin learning to live without you. I fear the easy part is over.

Leaning over his chair today
I went to place a kiss
Upon the place his head once rest
I wish that spot I'd missed

As I bent down his scent came up
Just as if he were there
I thought my heart would burst inside
And I would not have cared

I closed my eyes right then to pray
Oh Lord please let it be
That when I open up my eyes
His precious face I'll see

But when I looked he wasn't there
I knew he wouldn't be
But I discovered a way today
To keep him here with me

Questions for Grievers

Take some time now to think through, process, and write down
your responses to each of the questions below, as you go through
your own journey through spousal grief. Additional space is
provided below for you to record your answers.

1. Was the death of your spouse anticipated? If so, when your
   spouse died, how did you feel and was it how you thought
   you would feel? If not, what were your initial feelings? Did
   those feelings surprise you?

_____

_____

_____

_____

_____

_____

_____

_____

_____

_____

_____

_____

_____

_____

_____

_____

_____

_____

_____

2. Was the death of your spouse a sudden death? If so, how did you learn of the death? What was your first thought, your first feeling?

_____

_____

_____

_____

_____

_____

_____

_____

_____

_____

_____

_____

_____

_____

_____

_____

_____

_____

_____

_____

_____

_____

_____

_____

_____

3. What was the most difficult part of that first day?

_____

_____

_____

_____

_____

_____

_____

_____

_____

_____

_____

_____

_____

_____

_____

_____

_____

_____

_____

_____

_____

_____

_____

_____

_____

_____

_____

_____

_____

4. What type of service did you have? Did it help you begin the journey of grief?

_____

_____

_____

_____

_____

_____

_____

_____

_____

_____

_____

_____

_____

_____

_____

_____

_____

_____

_____

_____

_____

_____

_____

_____

_____

5. Looking back, is there something you wish you had done differently for the funeral service that would have helped you more?

_____

_____

_____

_____

_____

_____

_____

_____

_____

_____

_____

_____

_____

_____

_____

_____

_____

_____

_____

_____

_____

_____

_____

_____

_____

_____

_____

_____

After Everyone's Gone

Everyone's gone—day one alone. What now? Breathe. That's it, breathe. But why? If I breathe, I'll live, and if I live, I'll feel, and if I feel, I'll hurt, and if I hurt, I'll know this isn't a nightmare, and if I know this isn't a nightmare, then what? Breathing isn't for sissies.

Breathing is pretty overrated when you're grieving, and yet it's the one constant in a world of chaos. It is the only thing you absolutely can depend on not changing. Like it or not, you are going to breathe, which means you're going to live, going to feel, going to have to face the nightmare.

⁓ᴄₑ ₔᴐ⁓

My grief drapes over me like a shroud, and the weight of it takes my breath away. I am unnerved by the intensity of it and the way it clings to every fiber of my being as if it were taking up residence—or at least planning to stay for much too long. An unwelcome visitor this grief, and yet, I guess, a necessary one that I'll have to give shelter to for an undermined amount of time—and while doing so, learn from it things I never wanted to know. Things like, how many tears does it take to saturate a pillow, how many boxes of tissue can I go through in a day, is it possible to breathe while my body is racked with sobbing, and how long can I sob before I can't breathe and have to try and stop to get a breath? Or, is it possible to see out of eyelids that have ballooned to ten times their size with what seems like an eternity of crying but has only been one very long night? And, with all this crying, is it possible to take a drink of water without choking to death while taking the pill being offered for the headache that hurts from my heart? Strange lessons, unwanted lessons, life lessons that have no pass or fail grade, simply lessons. I hate this school.

⌐ ⌐⌐ ⌐⌐ ⌐

Grieving is horrible. It sends you down the black hole of despair. The hole is slick as greased lightning, and the trip to the bottom is short and swift. The problem with the black hole is that there are no handholds to help you climb out—and it takes a while to understand this. It takes a while to see that if you want out of the hole, you will need to carve out your own way. It's a decision only you can make, but you must make the decision if you're going to survive. It doesn't matter how much support you have; the bottom line is, you have to do it. No one else can do it for you. It's your journey.

However, I will let you in on a little secret. There is a rope in the hole. The rope is Jesus and the rope has handholds.

⌐ ⌐⌐ ⌐⌐ ⌐

What happened? We used to be together. We sat at the same table, ate the same food, watched the same TV shows, slept in the same bed, breathed the same air, and then you went away. Funny how that changes everything. I still sit at the same table, eat the same food, watch the same TV shows,

sleep in the same bed, and breathe the same air, but none of
it is the same.

⌒ ᥜ ᥬ ⌒

I sit alone encompassed by the heavy weight of nothing. No
thoughts, no feelings, no aches or pains—just a living, breath-
ing body sitting in a chair: a lump in a chair that takes up space
but is nonexistent. I don't care about anybody or anything. I
don't want to move, don't want to talk, don't want to see any-
one, don't want to eat or drink, don't want to do anything my
five senses can come up with. I just want to sit and let the world
pass me by. Maybe if I sit here long enough, I'll die.

⌒ ᥜ ᥬ ⌒

People come to comfort me and ask what they can do for me,
or what I need. I want to turn to them and quietly say, "Bring
him back." Can't they understand there is nothing they can do
for me except to return you *to* me?

⌒ ᥜ ᥬ ⌒

I saw a bumper sticker on a car today that said DEAD, and
under it was Drugs End All Dreams. *Wrong!* Death Ends All
Dreams. This is the place of no handholds. This is the place of
despair, the bottom of the hole, a place with nowhere to go but
up. Grab the rope.

⌒ ᥜ ᥬ ⌒

Thank you so much for the casserole . . . bang. Thank you so much for the beautiful plant . . . bang. Your outpouring of sympathy . . . bang. Each note written, each envelope addressed, each stamp placed is one more nail in the coffin of heartache. Is there nothing that isn't a heartache? And why do I have to thank you for being kind? Shouldn't you be that way without an expectation of a thank-you note? I'm suffering, and you expect a thank-you note. What's wrong with this picture?

⌐ ᵇᵉ ᵗⁱ⌐

It's *all* gone. Everything I had—my life, everything precious to me, everything that was mine, everything that was us—gone. And *I'm angry—terribly, terribly angry*, to the point of rage. And this rage is rolling out of my very being much like boiling water over the edge of a cauldron. I'm so angry with you right now for leaving me. I know, if you had the choice you would still be here, but it doesn't ease my anger. It eats at me. I can feel it churning inside me, my gut is on fire with it, and it has crept up into my heart which has turned into a white-hot coal that smolders in my chest. The slightest thought sets it ablaze, and heaven help me because this lays on me until I'm afraid I'll smother under the weight of it. And yet, I can't find a way to run from it or put it behind me, so I plod on day to day carrying the gargantuan burden that threatens to destroy me. Lord, help me!

⌐ ᵇᵉ ᵗⁱ⌐

Don't tell me what to do with his things! Who are you to tell me that the best thing for me to do is to get rid of everything so that I can forget and move on. *Forget?* Do you really think that removing everything about him and us will make me forget? Are you crazy? Do you really think that "out of sight, out of mind" works? How can you tell me what my heart needs to heal? When did you become the healing guru? You've never walked this path in my shoes—so understand that my heart will heal, but on its own terms, so keep your "you need to" to yourself and . . . *leave me alone!*

Ah, the anger. Not everyone will have anger. Some will miss this caustic emotion, but I didn't. Not only was I angry but I was empowered by it. It threatened to eat me alive and I couldn't shake it—and I didn't care. I wallowed in it and enjoyed it. And yet, I saw what it was doing to me. I wanted it gone but I didn't know how to let go. I felt like being angry gave me a purpose, a reason to live. In reality, it was destroying me and my ability to move on. Oh, how I needed something to cling to, to get me past the anger. And then I remembered the "rope in the hole," and the strength to go on that comes from grabbing hold of the rope.

Shaking—where did this uncontrollable shaking come from? Tears, tears, and shaking without end. Sobs that refuse to stop. How long will this go on?

So many emotions, so many things to take care of that seem like overwhelming tasks, so many decisions to be made about things I don't want to face right now. Why can't the world leave me alone for a while, to get my bearings, get my feet under me again? Why must I face these things now? Can't I be given just a little time to take a breath?

I am alone and I'm so afraid. I've lost so much with your death. It's not just the loss of my husband and friend. I've lost my protector—the one who always saw to it that I was safe from the world, the one who stepped in when I couldn't handle something and took care of it for me, the one I turned to for guidance when I didn't know what to do or how to do it, the one who was my emotional support, the one I leaned on. You were so strong when I was weak, and now there is no one to be strong for me. Now I have to handle the world all by myself, take care of things I know nothing about, and trust people I don't know to help me.

Before you, I wasn't like this. Before you, I was strong and capable and took on the world with confidence and determination. I made decisions and never looked back. Now, however, after years of you, I have lost that part of me and I am so afraid to take on the world again. I need you. I don't know who I am without you. I gave up "me" and became "us" when you came into my life—and now I'm not sure where the path is back to "me." I wonder if it will always be like this or if, in time, I'll find me again? I know that after all these years I won't be the same person I was. That leads me to wonder who I will find as I search for me. What if I don't like this "me" I find?

How many nights will I wander through this dark empty house? How many nights will I not sleep? How many tears will I have to cry before it starts to get better? What does it feel like to not hurt? Will there ever be a time when this is over?

I'm weary. Weary from tears, from not sleeping, not eating, thinking, remembering, living, living alone, living alone with all the burdens of decisions I don't want to make but have to. How easy it was when you were with me. All the tasks I do now with such difficulty I did then with no problem, because you were here. What makes the big difference? A bill is a bill, and it's the same bill it ever was. Why is your not being here when I must pay it such a major problem? I get out the checkbook, fill out the check, sign my name, put it in the envelope, and send it off. Exhaustion settles over my frazzled mind. I miss you.

Remembering—it's all I do anymore. I sit, close my eyes, and remember . . . everything. It's all I can do. There is no present or future, just the past—and it's become my present and future. But, maybe someday. . . .

The tears are falling once again
Do you think they'll ever stop
I can't remember when I've slept
I'm so tired that I could drop

Afraid to fall asleep at night
My heart begins to race
Am I strong enough to chance it
What if I see his face?

What if I hear his voice I love
Or think his scent I smell
What if I reach and he's not there
This fear is straight from hell

But what a comfort it would be
To see him one more time
To think I feel his arms again
The thought is so divine

But alas it just won't happen
Looks like I'll need a mop
The tears are falling once again
Do you think they'll ever stop?

Questions for Grievers

Take some time now to think through, process, and write down your responses to each of the questions below. Use the additional space provided below to record your answers.

1. How did you feel your first day alone?

_____

_____

_____

_____

_____

_____

_____

_____

_____

_____

_____

_____

_____

_____

_____

_____

_____

_____

_____

_____

_____

_____

_____

_____

2. How did you feel about God after your spouse died? Did
   your loss bring you closer to God, or move you further away
   from God? In either case, why?

_____

_____

_____

_____

_____

_____

_____

_____

_____

_____

_____

_____

_____

_____

_____

_____

_____

_____

_____

_____

_____

_____

_____

3. If your spouse's death moved you closer to God, share what that was like for you. How has that changed your faith?

_____

_____

_____

_____

_____

_____

_____

_____

_____

_____

_____

_____

_____

_____

_____

_____

_____

_____

_____

_____

_____

_____

_____

_____

_____

_____

_____

_____

4. If your spouse's death moved you away from God, share why.
   Do you still feel estranged from Him? What did you expect
   Him to do that He didn't do? Many are angry with God
   because He didn't answer prayer the way they wanted. Is it
   rational to expect an all-knowing God to answer in a way He
   knows isn't best for us just to spare us temporary pain?

_____

_____

_____

_____

_____

_____

_____

_____

_____

_____

_____

_____

_____

_____

_____

_____

_____

_____

_____

_____

_____

_____

5. There are so many emotions when we grieve. What ones are most difficult for you? How do you deal with them? Do you share your feelings with anyone?

_____

_____

_____

_____

_____

_____

_____

_____

_____

_____

_____

_____

_____

_____

_____

_____

_____

_____

_____

_____

_____

_____

_____

_____

_____

6. What did you do about your spouse's things? Did you get rid
   of everything immediately or keep things until you were less
   emotional? Looking back, do you feel your decision was the
   right one for you?

_____

_____

_____

_____

_____

_____

_____

_____

_____

_____

_____

_____

_____

_____

_____

_____

_____

_____

_____

_____

_____

_____

_____

_____

My Mind's Gone

I look at the confusion that engulfs me and it scares me. I really think I'm losing my mind. Every day is a challenge to not mess up something important by either forgetting what I'm doing, where something is, how to do it, or by not doing it twice. Paying big bills twice in one month takes a bite out of the budget— and, for some reason, the recipient never wants to give back the overpayment. However, confusion is normal, and I know it, so I just muddle through the best I can.

My mind is gone and I'm not sure I want it back, as I don't know where it's been. What kind of strange journey is it on, and why didn't it give me some notice that it was leaving? The audacity of it to just leave me without so much as a hint it was going. I would much rather my heart had left and taken the pain of your death with it—but maybe, my mind decided I should only deal with one thing at a time, and that grieving should be top priority. But doesn't my mind understand that its leaving just made the grieving harder? How can I concentrate on grieving when I can't concentrate? My mind is gone, and I wish I had gone with it.

My world is chaos. I have no mind. I can't think. I can't con-
centrate. I can't reason. What did you say to me? Where is my
mind? What is it you want? Do I even know how to do that? I
can't remember anything, and I hate this. I feel so vulnerable.
You're gone, and I've become totally inept and unable to make
even a simple decision—but no decision is simple anymore.
What is wrong with me?

I can't think, so I make a list to remember what I must do,
but I lose the list and must start over trying to remember what
was on it. And how am I going to make it tomorrow if I can't get
through today? I try to concentrate but can't, so again even the
simple things aren't simple. I try to hold a conversation and lose
my train of thought. I pick up my Bible; the words become a
jumble and my prayers are lost in all this confusion in my mind.

꩜

The inability to concentrate is driving me crazy. I absolutely
cannot focus on anything and I am afraid I'm literally losing
my mind. I have the attention span of an addled gnat and that's
on a good day! I am constantly double-checking everything I
do; misplacing things is so common it has become the norm.
I'm always making sure I check to see if I'm fully dressed before
going out the door, as I pay so little attention to what I'm doing
I'm afraid I'll show up somewhere in my pajamas. I know it's
normal, but it really worries me.

꩜

Oh, Lord, how do I do this? Each day is the beginning of eons
of time I must navigate with no direction or purpose, no ability

to make even simple decisions, no clear path to go down. I am so afraid, so lost, so incapable of anything. What little courage I have right now is knowing that you're holding me tight and I can't fall out of your grip.

It's just a stupid moment
I really can't say why
I think I'm going to laugh
Or maybe going to cry

My feelings are so awful
They treat me oh so bad
I never know what I'm to do
Be happy or be sad

I'm told that this is natural
That it will ease in time
But I think they are lying
I'm a clock without a chime

A book without a binding
With all the pages free
There's not one that is numbered
Is this person really me

My new life's so unsettled
I want the old one back
You see I am a widow
All I can see is black

Questions for Grievers

Take some time now to think through, process, and write down your responses to each of the questions below. Use the additional space provided below to record your answers.

1. How has the grieving process affected you mentally? How do you identify with the chaos described here?

_____

_____

_____

_____

_____

_____

_____

_____

_____

_____

_____

_____

_____

_____

_____

_____

_____

_____

_____

_____

_____

_____

2. All grievers do things and wonder if they are normal. What are some of the little things you do, or have done, and questioned the normalcy of them?

_____

_____

_____

_____

_____

_____

_____

_____

_____

_____

_____

_____

_____

_____

_____

_____

_____

_____

_____

_____

_____

_____

_____

3. Do you ever feel your mind has simply abandoned you? Is
   forgetfulness and/or confusion part of your daily struggle?
   How does this make you feel?

_____

_____

_____

_____

_____

_____

_____

_____

_____

_____

_____

_____

_____

_____

_____

_____

_____

_____

_____

_____

_____

_____

_____

_____

The Hardest Parts

I hate nights. Part of the problem is the bed—it's empty, it's cold, it's unwelcoming, and it's no longer ours. I have learned that if I take your pillow and put it to my back it gives me—if only for a short time—a false sense of comfort, as if I actually had you there, a moment to pretend all is well before reality laughs at me. I don't like reality. It cheats me of what I want: you.

I remember when we would cuddle together at night; I would put my head on your chest and listen to your heart beat and, occasionally, it would occur to me that one day I might not ever be able to hear that heart beat again. Well, that day has come. and listening to your heartbeat has become a memory I still hear.

Sheets . . . what do I do about the sheets? It's such a simple thing to take them off and wash them and put different ones on the bed. I know this, but it isn't a simple thing because the day you died we had spent the morning cuddling together and talking about our love for each other, and your pillowcase still has the scent of you; when I lay my head down at night and turn your way, ever so subtly your scent comes to me, and I close my eyes to the tears that spill down my face because I'm reliving that morning all over again. You're really not gone; it's just a cruel side of my imagination at work. But it isn't my imagination, and I'm back to: when will I be able to change the sheets?

～⤷᚜ ᚛⤶～

You know what's really hard? Never being touched. No one holding my hand, no kiss on the back of my neck, no hugs, no more long passionate kisses that end in such absolute intimacy. Oh, how I miss it all. In the beginning it was a very real problem. My loss made my desire for you escalate, and I didn't know how to handle it. So I turned it over to God, and asked Him to take away physical desire, and He did. That doesn't mean it totally went away; but when I feel the need rising, I call out to God and He blesses me by removing it. There are just so many things to learn to live without but—by God's amazing grace, it can be done, one thing at a time.

～⤷᚜ ᚛⤶～

I'm tired of people. I'm tired of being asked how I'm doing and giving the expected answer that I'm okay. I'm not okay, I'm a mess, life's horrible, the future looks bleak, and right now that's just the way it is. However, don't leave me—because I need you. Just don't ask how I'm doing, at least not today.

～⤷᚜ ᚛⤶～

Sometimes, when I'm alone, I hear your voice. Maybe you call my name, maybe just a random word, but I hear it. I know, I know . . . but I do hear it, and it's okay.

～⤷᚜ ᚛⤶～

I washed clothes today and I put in a shirt and pants that belonged to you, simply to be able to take them out of the washer and transfer them to the dryer, then out of the dryer and onto hangers and back to the closet. My clothes are so small; the laundry basket looks better with yours in there, too.

⌒ ⌒ ⌒

Come back. Come back and touch me. Wrap your arms around me, run your hands up and down my back and your fingers through my hair. Tilt my chin up one more time and look into my eyes as you bend your head to kiss me, just one more time.

⌒ ⌒ ⌒

You died alone. That really bothers me. I think about what must have gone through your mind as you knew what was happening . . . or did you have time to know? A massive heart attack, as you died of, can be immediate or give you precious seconds to understand what is happening. I think you had time to know because of how I found you. What makes me cry the most is, I know your last thought was of me. Everything you ever did was aimed at taking care of me. Now my first thought is always of you.

I remember you saying to me that it didn't matter what the world thought about me, as long as you liked what you saw. Now you're not here. Does the world matter now?

⌒ ⌒ ⌒

I'm *screaming* on the inside! Can't you hear me? The sound is deafening and you're oblivious. *Listen to me.* Draw me out. Don't let me keep this inside. *Help me!*

〜⌒ᒉ 𝕫⌒〜

I'm beginning to have a love-hate relationship with this space called my closet. On one side are my clothes, on the other side are yours, and the floor is His. My side is a moot point, but your side keeps me reeling, while His gives me healing.

I open the door to this space; my eyes are drawn immediately to your clothes, and the ritual begins. First, I look at them hanging there, unused, no longer moved from place to place as they're worn, washed, and returned. Next, I grab as many as I can get my arms around and bury my face in them and hug them to me and feel the tears begin to trickle down my face as my breath catches and the sobs begin. Often, when I'm finished sobbing over your clothes I go to your dresser and open the drawer that still holds your underwear and run my hands over it just to hold on a little longer. Your underwear drawer always had a different scent than mine and I lean over it and breathe in that scent and sob a little while longer, then return to the closet. Usually by this time, my grief is inconsolable, so I shut the closet door behind me, turn off the light, and go on my face before God and pour it all out. Why, you ask, have I given God the closet floor? Because it's the one place of quiet where pets can't reach me, and where all sounds are muffled, but where I can cry as loudly as I want—and in my grief, humble myself before Him. In this place on the floor I am able to come to an inner peace, as He wraps His arms around me and lets me grieve.

〜⌒ᒉ 𝕫⌒〜

Talk to me; mundane nothingness will do. Just break the silence of my world—but can you go away while you do it because, much as I want to hear you, I want to be alone and I don't know how to do both at the same time.

You died on Wednesday, and I feel my life is being defined by Wednesdays. Wednesday, one week ago today, Wednesday, two weeks ago today, Wednesday, three weeks ago today, and on and on it goes. Will I ever again be able to face a Wednesday without dread or tears? It doesn't make any sense. It's just a day. No, it's the day my world came crashing down around me.

I hate the word "today." I hate the word "today" because I don't want to live in today. Today means I'm alone. Today means my dreams are shattered. Today means reality, and I hate reality. I much prefer "yesterday." Yesterday encompasses years of time. Yesterday means being able to see you, touch you, hear you, smell you, and taste the joy of being with you. Yesterday means us. I love yesterday.

I looked at an old Victorian home in a magazine today and my eyes were riveted to the "widow's walk" at the top of the house. My heart cried out to all the women who had paced that narrow path of eternity searching through the mists of nature and tearful eyes for a glimpse of the ship that would never return. It may not be at the top of a house, but I too am pacing and waiting, knowing you'll never return.

The little things are killing me
Don't really have a clue
On what the protocol is here
On what I am to do

Am I supposed to put it up
Or can it stay right there
I do not want to move one thing
This really isn't fair

His clothes are in the closet
His shoes beside his chair
How long before I'm able
To move them anywhere

Have thought about these things a lot
Know I can't make a shrine
But I don't have to move them yet
I'm going to take my time

When I feel I am stronger
I'll start with a few things
That I don't think I'll miss too much
See what the next day brings

When I feel I am stronger
I'll think on this some more
But right now I can't face it
It's just too big a chore.

Questions for Grievers

Take some time now to think through, process, and write down your responses to each of the questions below. Use the additional space provided below to record your answers.

1. What's the hardest part of your grieving? Why?

_____

_____

_____

_____

_____

_____

_____

_____

_____

_____

_____

_____

_____

_____

_____

_____

_____

_____

_____

_____

_____

_____

_____

2. Do you feel you are healing? If not, what could you do differently to change your life for the positive?

_____

_____

_____

_____

_____

_____

_____

_____

_____

_____

_____

_____

_____

_____

_____

_____

_____

_____

_____

_____

_____

_____

_____

_____

3. For some people, after the death of a spouse, sexual desire is
   a hard thing to handle. If you are struggling with this, how
   are you handling it—and is it helping? Have you thought of
   turning it over to God?

_____

_____

_____

_____

_____

_____

_____

_____

_____

_____

_____

_____

_____

_____

_____

_____

_____

_____

_____

_____

_____

_____

_____

Regrets, Depression, and the Hand of God

I know that some people who read this either have no faith in God or don't know the one true God of the Bible. You have no idea how that distresses me; I can't imagine how they're going to get through their time of grief. Who will they lean on? Whose hand will they hold who will never let them go? Who will carry them and never put them down? To whom do they go with all the things too private to share? Who will they turn to here on earth who will never disappoint them?

The answers to these questions all begin and end with Jesus. For with Jesus, I have a savior who loved me so much He came to me. Awesome.

～ ⌣ ⸙ ⁓ ⸜ ～

I have come to my special place to be alone with God and put before Him all the things I can't deal with. I sit here waiting for the words to come but nothing happens, so I sit awhile longer, and still nothing. The tears are now softly falling and still no words come; I begin rocking back and forth with my arms wrapped around my knees and I hear a small sound coming from deep within me, but no words. It's often like this when I come before Him, because my grief is so intense that I can't form words to describe it and the beauty of it is that I don't have to, for the Bible tells me the Holy Spirit will make intercession for me with groanings that cannot be uttered. I fall on my face before my God and give it all over to the Holy Spirit to voice my pain.

There is something about this time I spend on my face before my God that is so spellbinding. As I am physically on the floor of my closet, I am spiritually at the feet of Jesus, and I know that if I just open my eyes I would see Him, but I don't need to because I know He is there and hearing every word. As usual, when my time with Him comes to a close, I find I am strengthened and able to face the world again.

❦

I find myself thinking about the strangest things these days. Watching you walk away from me, I would always notice that one of your shoulders was just a little lower than the other. I'm not sure I remember which shoulder it was, and I'm not sure why I even think about it, but I do, and it bothers me that I can't remember which shoulder was lower. I don't like it that I can't remember. If I had died, what would you forget about me? The little things are sometimes the biggest things. Stumbling blocks everywhere I look.

❦

I am a prisoner of my own making, captured by the swirling of my restless mind that refuses to leave you alone. I live in a world of constant memories, and you're alive and well in everything. I take a shower, and the towel I'm using is one you once used, and I cling to it. I stand in front of my sink and find my eyes drifting to your empty one. I open the closet door and you are there in your clothes that still hang there waiting. I feed the pets and look into the dull eyes of your beloved dog who mourns for you as I do. I walk to the mailbox and pull out the letters that are still addressed to you. Every step I take, everything I see, feel, hear, taste, and touch is alive with a memory of you, and the memories just keep coming.

I find my mind wandering back to the first day we met and dredging up things I haven't thought of in years; they ramble around in my head, then dash straight to my wounded heart. I remember hearing a song with a line that said, "the first word in memory is me," and how true it is—for everything says, remember me. I do.

It's amazing the things that surface with death. Things that are better off forgotten and buried in the past are now rearing their ugly heads and sneering at me, and I seem to be drowning in the soup of regret. How do I get past this?

I know everyone has regrets and that all marriages, no matter how good, are full of them, but it doesn't make dealing with my own regrets any easier. I seem to be wearing them like a horsehair shirt and, adding to the soup of regret, a bunch of "what ifs" and "if onlys" which just gives me a taste of humanity I don't seem to be able to stomach.

I know that if I had died instead of you, you would now be dealing with your own set of regrets—and I know what a lot of them would be—but that doesn't make it any easier on me now. The fact is, I didn't die, so here I am not only grieving over your death but also grieving over fragmented little bits of our lives— little bitty nothings that now eat at me, keep me up at night, and cause rivers of tears.

But as I write this, I'm beginning to realize something I hadn't thought of before: If I had died, I would have forgiven you for anything and everything because I wouldn't have wanted you to cry over one single thing. Even if I had died suddenly and alone, as you did, without time to tell you, I would still want you to somehow know it was all okay. I would want you to remember all the good times and bury the regrets when you buried me. If I had died first, I would have wanted you to do nothing but to remember me, not the regrets. So sweetheart, that's exactly what I'm going to do. I'm going to curl up in your chair and ask your forgiveness one last time, bury the regrets, and remember you.

⁀ ⌣ ⌐ ⥩ ⌐ ⁀

Oh loneliness, leave me alone! I can't bear living with you one more second of one more day. Don't you know what you're doing to me? Don't you know how you make me feel? Don't you care?

I am a loner by nature. I have always enjoyed my own company, even as a child, preferring my room and a good book to the neighborhood kids. I have never, absolutely never, understood how anyone could be lonely, or how it felt to be lonely—until now. Now I understand, and I know that through all the grieving process, this one little emotion is the one that will come the closest to destroying me. I have no words to adequately describe what this feels like, but I can say that it is an immense emptiness that pervades every cell in my body. It renders me incapable of being at peace anywhere I go or with anything I do because no matter how many people I'm around, or how busy I am, it is never enough. I'm miserable home alone and I'm miserable with people. Wherever I go I want to be somewhere else, and I'm always searching for something I can't find. The peace and quiet I once loved about our home has become a prison and, as I sit here staring blankly and absorbing the incessant noise of the television I'm not watching, my mind is spinning around trying to find something to cling to while my heart is, well, still beating.

Loneliness is such an abstract thing. It has no dimensions but fills every space, can be felt but not seen, consumes my time but is timeless; however, the one ray of hope is it that will have an end, just not soon enough.

I was told shortly after you died to be careful not to make a "shrine" out of anything that was yours. At the time, I didn't really understand that sage bit of advice, but today it smacked me in the face. It dawned on me that the drawer that holds your hairbrush, comb, cologne, etc. has become a huge stumbling block, as it smells like you. I have gone so far as to put a small stool in front of the bathroom counter so I can sit down, open that drawer, close my eyes, and breathe you in. I have begun to come to this drawer much too often and often come to it before I go to the Lord in prayer. In other words, this drawer has become a "shrine."

How easily my grieving put a stumbling block before me. How easy to lean on something tangible to ease this emotional turmoil. It isn't that breathing in your scent is a sin but it's the idea that it has taken such an important place in my heart, setting itself up to take precedence over everything else. Constantly sitting here breathing you in is keeping me from letting go. How can I let go when I can't walk away from this drawer that keeps you ever-present?

Now I understand about shrines. So, here comes the hard part as I take everything out of the drawer, box it up, and put it away. I'm not ready to get rid of it and I may never get rid of it, and that's OK, but as of today the "shrine" comes down. Dear Lord, give me the strength to not rebuild this shrine.

I'm not a coffee drinker, but you were; your day didn't start until you had that first cup of coffee. How I loved the smell of it in the morning, and I always told you that I didn't know how anything could smell so good and taste so bad. You would laugh and tell me I just didn't know what was good; but I did know that drinking pots of it all day, every day, wasn't good for you and I'd fuss with you about how much you drank. That coffee pot on the counter became a major source of irritation to me. Now, however, that coffee pot I so desperately wanted to put away then is still where you left it when you left me. I get up every morning, and the first thing I see when I come into the kitchen is that coffee pot, sitting there alone, unused, waiting, no longer filling the house with the aroma of freshly brewed coffee but rather serving as a grim reminder of you. Mornings don't smell so good anymore.

Today, I decided it was time to pick up the area around your chair, because I had become suspicious that I was making a shrine out of it. I started with your shoes, picking them up and hugging them against me like a baby as I walked them to the closet, to put them with the rest of your clothes—and crying all the way to the bedroom because I shouldn't be doing this, you should—then going back to your chair to see what else I could move. It wasn't so much the chair as the table beside it that caused so much pain, for on that table were all the little things that made up so many memories: the Zebra brand ink pen you always carried, the innumerable business cards, the toothpicks you were never without that rode so comfortably in your shirt pocket or the side of your mouth. Why did you have so many toothpicks, anyway? The table was covered with little bits and pieces of you but, no matter how much I saw, everything paled in comparison to one thing: your coffee cup. That cold, empty coffee cup was my undoing. It just sat there in silence screaming at me and I heard every word, "Hey honey, will you fill up my coffee cup?" "How about another cup of coffee?" "Is there any coffee left?" "Will you stop nagging me about how much coffee I drink?" Then silence—deafening silence.

I'm not sure how it happened but the next thing I realized, I was curled up in a ball in your chair, cradling that coffee cup in my hands—and this time the sounds I heard were not deafening silence but an internal wailing that was coming from somewhere deep inside me and thundering against the walls, and I was helpless to stop it. I don't know how long I stayed there but I think it was several hours, or possibly minutes; I don't really know. I do know that when it was over, for the first time I felt like I was beginning to accept the fact you were never coming

back and that I was going to have to go through the rest of my
life without you. It was a step—small, but a step.

❧ ❦ ❧

I've been avoiding places with lots of people, church being
the one exception. But today I went to the mall for some insig-
nificant thing and somewhere in the crowd I heard a man's voice
that sounded so much like yours. My eyes raced toward the
direction of the sound, my heart gasped—and as usual, when
confronted with the overwhelming thought of you, I cried.
How long will this go on?

❧ ❦ ❧

The mail came today as usual, and as usual there were so many
things addressed to Mr. and Mrs. Don't these people know there
is no Mister here anymore? Why are they so determined to keep
reminding me of your absence, punishing me with my loss, and
why can't I let them know? Why—because being able to see
"Mr." on the mail I receive keeps me connected with you just a
little longer.

❧ ❦ ❧

Why didn't anyone tell me what this would be like? Why didn't
anyone tell me what it would be like to live with a broken
heart, a mind that is useless, tears that are nonstop, and that
I would be on an emotional rollercoaster that had no appar-
ent end? Why didn't anyone tell me what it would be like to
get up in the morning more tired than when I went to bed,

and that everything in the house would hold a memory that would reduce me to sobbing? Why didn't anyone tell me that doing something for the first time, that I last did with you, would bring me to my knees with grief, and that you would be in every thought, every movement, every object? Why didn't anyone tell me that no matter how hard I prayed or how long I stood there looking down the hall, you would never again come out of our bedroom and walk down that empty hall to me? Why didn't anyone tell me how empty a bed can be and how desolate and empty a house can be? Why didn't anyone tell me these things?

Night is coming, and that frightens me. It's not the dark but the quiet that surrounds me and allows me to hear the ramblings of my restless mind and the crying of my heart. Day is busy with physical things that keep my body moving, but night is busy with emotional things that keep my head and heart moving in ways that are far more exhausting than the physical could ever be. I struggle to turn my mind off so my heart won't respond, but it's impossible. All I want is the sleep that doesn't come until exhaustion overwhelms me.

Night is so hard. I'm hoping that one day, as my grief ebbs, the night will become a time of precious memories that will give me comfort as I remember our life together, but I'm afraid that day is lightyears away, if ever. It's too soon to think about tomorrow, so for now I will tiptoe toward the night, hoping this time it won't see me.

One of the worst parts of your dying is you're not here to get me through it. You've always been my strength in times of trouble or grief. Now, during the most horrible time of my life, you aren't here. Who will walk me through this? Whose arms will encircle me, and whose chest will I lay my head against as the tears come? Who will cuddle me at night and tell me it will be all right? Who, if not you?

I have found, since you died, that people are very uncomfortable with death. When they ask about my husband, and I tell them that you recently died, they all seem to come up with the same stupid "I'm sorry," when you know they probably aren't sorry at all. They didn't know you; your dying means nothing to them. So, why don't they say something meaningful instead? What, you ask, should that be? Oh, I don't know—how about, "I'm sorry"?

I've done it again! I've managed to get in the car and end up where I was going with absolutely no recollection of getting there. This really frightens me because, if I can't remember being on the road, am I even paying any attention to what I'm doing? How much of a danger am I to others? Even when I try to focus while driving I find, more often than not, that I get lost in my thoughts and that the road becomes a winding ribbon of gray that I'm magically gliding over—to come to a destination on a trip my mind didn't take.

It's one of those days when I have nothing to do, but I need to find something—because I find myself adrift in a sea of memories that threaten to drag me under, and the depression I'm battling is covering me again. I haven't done anything about fighting it and I'm not sure why. Maybe I like wallowing in it because, as long as it holds me so tightly, I don't have to move in any direction, and that seems safe and easy. It's so tiring making decisions and I don't want to. Some days the hardest decision is just the one to get out of bed, and sometimes I don't make that decision until it's almost time to go back to bed.

I find sleep to be such a wonderful escape. I've also found that I've become an expert sleeper—and in a small way that frightens me. Too bad it doesn't frighten me enough to do something about it.

One step at a time, one step at a time, if I hear one step at a time again, I think I'll shoot the messenger. The problem is, the messenger is right. It *is* one small step at a time, and sometimes the step is backward instead of forward—but even backward moves me forward. I find that, stumble as I may, I eventually move on and that what I couldn't do last week, or even yesterday, I'm handling better today . . . one step at a time.

Last night I dreamed about you for the first time since you died. It's been something I've dreaded, and wanted, and it happened.

A stupid dream except for the end—you said, "I love you." Not such a stupid dream after all.

I've been wandering through the house today, going from room to room, picking things up and putting them down and picking them up again. Funny how things we lived with for so long have become so new to me. I went through your drawers just to touch your things, socks, shorts, t-shirts—you know, your stuff. I'm afraid my tears got some things wet, but I guess that's okay. I don't know what to do with them since I can't wear them, but I can't let go of them either. What would you do, in my place?

I've grown tired of being a crybaby. I've grown tired of tears, sadness, depression, anxiety, frustration, low self-esteem, fear, insecurity, and all the other negative emotions I've been battling, but I'm too tired to do anything with them. Will someone please come get them?

I have decided I have to do something about the depression that has engulfed me. I'm off to the doctor, to fill his ear with my emotional status and ask for the help I need but don't want. I really have mixed emotions about this, but I can't go on under this black cloud forever and I'm having a difficult time chasing it away. There is a side of me that would really like to get through this. I guess that's the side that's winning—which, in itself, gives me hope. A tiny ray of hope that is gently nudging me on.

⌁ ⌁ ⌁

I'm not hungry, so why do I have to eat? I don't want it. I don't want to cook it. I don't want to eat it. I don't want to clean up the mess. I'm just not interested at all.

Cooking has never been one on of my favorite things. I've always referred to it as a survival skill—and little did I know how right I was. How do you cook for one? Everything comes packaged in two or more. Why do packagers do that when I'm not going to eat two pork chops—when I'm struggling to choke down one? And why can't they package a half pound of ground beef instead of a whole pound? I know there is some efficient person out there yammering about freezing the rest of it, but why would I want to freeze part of it when I don't want any of it to begin with?

And if I should decide to cook something, or even bring in something already cooked, I have no desire to eat it. I don't want to look at it on a plate, don't want to look at it in a box, don't want it from a plastic carry-out container, and don't want it from a bag. I simply don't want it. The problem is, now that I have it, I have to do something with it but what? "Eat it," you say. *You* eat it.

⌁ ⌁ ⌁

I'm restless. Today is one of those days when I do nothing but roam around the house, going from room to room looking out the windows and seeing nothing. My mind as well as my body is restless, and I have no idea what I want to do or where I want to go—and if I did want to go somewhere, there's no one to go with me. I know I have lots of things that need to be done but I don't want to do them, and I really don't care if they get done or not. I feel sort of displaced, like I don't belong anywhere, kind of like a kite that is blown and tossed by the wind with no control of its own. On these days, I find my emotions are pretty volatile. I run the gamut from numbness to hysterical crying, but nothing seems to last long, as each room I enter brings on a different set of memories and emotions.

Looking out a window to the backyard makes me cry, as I look at the grass you used to cut with such precision and the rather helter-skelter job I do. The ducks waddling through the yard make me cry because we used to have such fun feeding them and laughing at their antics when a few pieces of bread broke the parade route and caused such quacking and dashing to catch the closest tidbit.

It's always the little things that trigger me, and when I get through crying over something I move on to the next room, which may bring a totally different feeling. I'm just amazed at how much time I can use up wandering around doing nothing, but in a sense it isn't nothing—for each room I enter, each tender memory that is touched, and each response that follows is another step to healing. I know someday I'll emerge from this grief and life will be different and it's something I look forward to. But for now, aimless wandering is the best I can do today.

❧

The depression is better, and I'm now glad I did something about it. Don't for a minute think it has relieved me of my grief, but it has helped me to walk with it better. The tears are still there and my heart hurts just the same, but there is a difference I can't quite put my finger on. Possibly it has enabled me to use my grief instead of letting my grief use me. In doing so, I am able to start moving on instead of standing still. I guess it doesn't really matter much why or how I am helped by the antidepressant—just that I am and that's enough.

Remember me for I am one
As you climb the stairs to your room
As you lay your head on his shoulder
As your hands then lips touch

Remember me for I am one
As you stroll down the sidewalk
Looking in windows
Stroll through the park

Remember me for I am one
As you sit quietly before the fire
Eyes meeting with gentle smiles
Surrounded by peace together

Remember me for I am one
As you plan your dinner party
Setting the table for an even number
Just once could it be odd

Remember me for I am one
In a culture that values two
I sit alone forgotten
My world no longer paired

Questions for Grievers

Take some time now to think through, process, and write down your responses to each of the questions below. Use the additional space provided below to record your answers.

1. What do you remember most about your spouse?

_____

_____

_____

_____

_____

_____

_____

_____

_____

_____

_____

_____

_____

_____

_____

_____

_____

_____

_____

_____

_____

_____

_____

2. All marriages have regrets. What are yours, and how are you
   handling them?

_____

_____

_____

_____

_____

_____

_____

_____

_____

_____

_____

_____

_____

_____

_____

_____

_____

_____

_____

_____

_____

_____

_____

_____

3. "What if" and "if only" cause us so much pain. Do you have
   a "what if" or "if only" you are struggling with? What are
   you doing to help yourself let go of it?

   _____

   _____

   _____

   _____

   _____

   _____

   _____

   _____

   _____

   _____

   _____

   _____

   _____

   _____

   _____

   _____

   _____

   _____

   _____

   _____

   _____

   _____

   _____

   _____

   _____

   _____

4. There are only two things you can do with grief: You can
   wallow in it the rest of your life, or you can make the choice
   to work it through and move on. What are you doing with
   your grief?

_____

_____

_____

_____

_____

_____

_____

_____

_____

_____

_____

_____

_____

_____

_____

_____

_____

_____

_____

_____

_____

_____

_____

_____

5. Have you met loneliness? If so, describe how it feels to you. How are you dealing with it? If it is gone, how long was it with you and when did you realize it was gone?

_____

_____

_____

_____

_____

_____

_____

_____

_____

_____

_____

_____

_____

_____

_____

_____

_____

_____

_____

_____

_____

_____

_____

_____

_____

6. Is depression a problem for you? What are you doing about
it? If nothing, why aren't you getting help?

_____

_____

_____

_____

_____

_____

_____

_____

_____

_____

_____

_____

_____

_____

_____

_____

_____

_____

_____

_____

_____

_____

_____

_____

_____

_____

The Four-Letter Word "Widow," and the Beginning of Healing

I've decided that the word "widow" is a four-letter word—one which comes only after the word "dead" in terms of the degree of devastation to what once was a pretty good life. In the time it takes to catch a very short breath, the rest of one's life is inexplicably altered and never is the same again. From that one moment on and for a long time to come, everything is measured by that one horrible moment when the world stood still.

It's one hour, it's one day, it's one week, one month, one year . . . and oh yes, time heals everything, so I go on with life and wait for that magical day when time heals, but what is "it" that causes the healing? I suppose it must be my heart, but how could it be when my heart shattered into so many tiny pieces that they couldn't possibly be found and restored to what they once were? Or maybe it's my mind—but it can't be that, because I'd need to have one in order for time to heal it and, be it a blessing or a curse or both, my mind started running on autopilot. Somehow I made it from day to day without thinking, because thinking would have just heightened the pain, so that's not "it." Whatever "it" is, it's very elusive, and "it" doesn't have the decency to show its face so that, for just a moment, I might see even a tiny dot of light through all the black.

Funny how my life stopped, and yet the rest of the world just kept on going as if nothing had ever happened. Oh, for a while people hovered around me, the cards and calls were non-stop, and I felt like the front door was always in the process of opening or closing; but one day I noticed that the phone hadn't rung as much, and then the mailbox wasn't so full, and the front door hadn't let anyone in. It was once again life as usual—their life as usual, not mine.

I grew tired. I joined a grief support group, a book club, volunteered at the local whatever, and tried to keep busy. I also learned to hate the phrase, "if you keep busy, 'it' makes every-thing easier." *When? How?* and *Why* doesn't "it" do it *now?* I began to become very cynical about "it." I began to chase "it" like you would a butterfly—only this butterfly couldn't be seen, so I began to look over, under, and around, and still found nothing.

Then one day, I looked up—and realized that I'd made it until ten in the morning and that there were no constant tears. A few days or weeks went by, and I'd made it until noon, then three, then six. Then one day somewhere in time, I realized that I had made it one whole day without sobbing all day, and then one whole day with only minor tears—and then the day came when I hadn't cried at all, and I realized that as painful as it was, I was going to survive and that "it" had done whatever "it" does. And I began to understand exactly what "it" is.

It was precisely at the moment of realization of what "it" is that I began to look back on all the old trite sayings I had begun to hate, and thought about all the hours I spent in prayer and how helpless I was physically, mentally, emotionally, and spiri-tually. It was then that I realized that "it" was with me all along, even though I couldn't see Him and I had to go through the black to finally come to this moment—the moment when I discovered that I couldn't find Him because He was carrying me.

⌒ ↶ ↷ ⌒

All my life I've heard, "Time heals all wounds." The funny thing is, time doesn't heal anything. The only thing time does is give you a space in your life to make decisions about how you're going to carry on. I learned one thing when you died, and that was, I could wallow in my grief the rest of my life or I could *choose* to work through it. I must admit I mulled over the possibility of wallowing forever, because it was easy to do; wallowing takes absolutely no effort. But I couldn't bear the thought of going through the rest of my life crying and depressed. Who wants to do that? Not me.

(As I write this, my mother has recently died and been buried. I remember standing with my dad by the casket and having some of her friends come up to pay their respects. One of them quietly made the comment that Mother would be mortified to know this was an open-casket funeral because it absolutely was not what she wanted. I remember turning to her friend and saying that a funeral is not for the dead but for the living, and whatever it takes to get my dad through it is exactly what would be done. Truthfully, I hadn't thought about it until that moment, but when you died, that was exactly what I did— whatever it took to get us through it.)

⌒ ↶ ↷ ⌒

I was told, sometime during the beginning of my widowed state, that everything would get better in increments of six weeks. I thought it was a crazy thing to say, because I couldn't see how six weeks could change me—but somehow, it indeed works that way. The first six weeks were so devastating that I couldn't breathe.

By the end of the next six weeks it had become three months. I couldn't believe you had been gone three months and that I was still relatively sane, or at least functioning on some primal level. And now, here I am at more than four-and-a-half months and heading toward six, and I can't imagine it's been almost half a year.

The idea that I have almost one-half a year behind me causes me to reflect on all the changes I've come through. I still mourn for you daily. The tears are there at a moment's notice and I still find myself crying when I walk through the canned vegetable section of the grocery store, because it reminds me of when you'd come with me and pick out all the things you wanted for your awesome vegetable soup that I can't remember how to make, which makes me cry more because I'll never taste it again. However, even with this daily mourning, I have noticed that I am beginning to, if not laugh, at least chuckle occasionally—and I am slowly, very slowly, beginning to see the world around me again. People are still exasperating, and I have so much trouble being patient with them, and I just want to hang a sign around my neck that says, "Widow—Handle with Care!" They should know I'm not okay, but since they don't know about you I have to be sensitive to their insensitivity—precisely because they *don't* know.

I am also finding out, at almost six months, that I'm beginning to think—and let me stress the word *think*—about what to do about your things. I still go into the closet and hold your clothes and cry and I don't know when I'll be able to let them go, but it won't be until I'm ready to do it. I still remember the time I moved your chair, three months after you died, and the emotional upheaval and the hurry to put it back. What a personal thing grief is—and I just realized I'm writing this as if you're going to be reading it. Almost six months and you're still such a part of me I write to you.

⌒ ⌒⌐ ⌐⌐⌒

Life is going on and today, for the first time, I felt like I might want to join in—not too much, just a little to see how it feels and to see whether I can handle it. The six-weeks thing is still applicable. I still cry, but not every day, and not over the same things—which, I guess, is a kind of moving on. I find I can pay the bills most of the time without thinking about it; and I made it through the grocery store without tears, but barely. My heart still aches in ways I didn't know hearts could and it's still awful, but I keep pushing on. I still miss you so much that it takes my breath away, and at the same time there's a part of me that never wants that to change and a part of me that wishes it would. I have a hard time with the thought of ever letting you go and I don't know if I ever really will. There is something so safe about keeping you near. I always felt safe with you because it didn't matter what happened, you'd take care of it. You were larger than life to me and now that you're gone, there's no one to keep me safe—and that, in itself, frightens me. What a sniveling coward I've become without you. I was so strong before we met and I handled life so easily, but not now, not after all the years of leaning on you and depending on you. I don't like this feeling of fear—or maybe it's not exactly fear—but whatever it is, I don't like it. Oh, how I need you by my side. So much for joining life again.

⌒ᴄᴇ ᷔᴐ⌒

How long has it been since God called you home? It's been a lifetime to me but, to my surprise, I'm making it without you and learning to go from day to day, putting one foot in front of the other and plodding along. Today I actually smiled about something, so I guess there's hope. Maybe one day I'll truly laugh, but I think that day is pretty far off. I was amazed that the smiling wasn't immediately followed by tears. Hmm, maybe this is what they call surviving?

⌒ᴄᴇ ᷔᴐ⌒

Our daughter thinks that my grief is getting the best of me and she's worried. It's been almost a year and she thinks I should be moving a little further along in the grieving process. Even though I tell her I'm okay, she doesn't believe me. She thinks I cry far too much, and maybe I do, but I cry for you. No, that's not right. I might as well be honest: I cry for me, because I don't have you. The problem isn't me but her. She doesn't wear my grief and doesn't understand that it may be almost a year to her but it's yesterday to me. I'm surviving—what more does she expect?

⌒ᴄᴇ ᷔᴐ⌒

I'm here—not too sure where here is, but I'm here. It's a place somewhere between heartache and healing, and I'm not too sure what to do with this place. I find I'm struggling with moving on, as if doing so might eradicate you from my heart, and although I know that's impossible, it still frightens me; and yet, I am developing a need to move on because I've become worn out with grieving. I am beginning to yearn for more, but I'm still having trouble reaching out; it requires stepping away from what was, to enter what could be—and that makes me uncomfortable.

I am at a place where I can essentially start over and make my life anything I want, but the sadness of doing it alone keeps me anchored where I am. This is a place of constant reflection on past, present, and future, with thoughts and emotions bouncing off my heart like a ball off the side of a house. I am torn from all sides as I struggle with this next hurdle in the process of healing and the challenge it brings for me to now step out and have a life. Hmm, maybe that's the issue—not in having a life, but in having a life alone.

Today, I'm strong. Today, I awoke without tears. Today, I got up, got dressed, combed my hair, and put on makeup. Today will be better than yesterday. Today, I will be okay—not good but okay.

Today, I just lost it all as I walked into the living room and saw your dog with his head on the seat of your chair, eyes closed, grieving. Today, he and I will cry together. But tomorrow. . . .

I awoke this morning without tears, a milestone that I managed to continue until I made it to the kitchen, but still a good thing.

Maybe tomorrow will be even better, and wouldn't it be great to finally begin to awaken every day with dry eyes?

~⊂∼ ∼⊃~

Today is Friday—and I just realized I missed a Wednesday. It's the first Wednesday since you died that I haven't counted in some form or fashion.

~⊂∼ ∼⊃~

I forgive you. I forgive you for all the times you hurt my feelings, made me angry, made me sad, and for falling off the pedestal I placed you on—but most of all, I forgive you for dying and leaving me alone. It's taken me a long time to forgive you for that, but I have. The white-hot rage I felt after you died slowly cooled and turned into a quieter anger—then, over time, the smoldering coals finally burned themselves out. I guess it's part of the acceptance of death and moving on and another step toward healing but, whatever the reason, I'm glad to see it gone.

I also forgive me. I forgive me for hurting your feelings, making you angry, making you sad, and for falling off the pedestal you placed me on. I believe that forgiving me has been just as hard as forgiving you, for it's so hard to look at my own mistakes and the regrets from those mistakes and to come to an acceptance of my shortcomings. But I have. We were just two people who loved each other and did the best we could with who we were.

~⊂∼ ∼⊃~

I find it almost impossible to believe that it's going on a year. I say almost, because the road has been so long and the battle to survive so intense that it has had to be a long time. On the other hand, there are times—most of the time, really—when it still seems like yesterday. I don't cry all day anymore, but I still have tears on most days and it doesn't take much to bring the tears rolling down my face. Usually it's over something sweet, but occasionally I revert back to the gut-wrenching sobs of the beginning—and that's okay, too. After all these months, I've just quit worrying if all the tears are normal or not and just let them flow. I know I'm healing and that's all I care about. Healing has no time frame.

Yesterday was the first anniversary of your death. It was a good day, and it was a bad day. I missed you so much yesterday as I thought back on a year ago; tears were everywhere, and last night was rough, but today it is different. Today, I awoke with a sense of peace that I was going to be okay. I still have a very long, hard road ahead, but I have come through all the "firsts" and survived each one of them: our anniversary, Valentine's Day, my birthday, your birthday, Thanksgiving, Christmas, New Year's Day—days that were sad and lonely and difficult, but I made it. I made it and it feels really good. I am a survivor! I have been to the brink of despair and I'm very slowly coming back, and I'm going to be okay.

It is amazing, absolutely amazing, as I look back on this past year. Baby steps, tiny wobbly baby steps on spaghetti legs that ever-so-slowly changed to where I am today and, through it all, I look back and know I was never alone. I rested on God's promise that He would now be my provider and protector, and He was. When I thought my heart would break and I wouldn't be able to draw another ragged breath, He was there. When the daily decisions of life were overwhelming, He was there. When I felt deserted by the world, He was there to support me.

How often I read and reread the "Footprints" poem and clung to the last sentence that said, "It was then that I carried you"—and He has. As I stood tottering on the edge of the black hole of despair and cried out, He picked me up and cuddled me close and whispered in my ear that He had me and that, although I would have to make my way down the road of grief, I would never be alone, for He would never put me down until I was strong enough. When I was stronger, He began putting me down to build my strength—and picked me up again when I would stumble. We now walk hand in hand, but He is still there to catch me when I'm weak. One day, I will come to the place where a hand on my shoulder will be all I need. It has been a long, exhausting walk, but I have learned that I can face anything, because I face nothing alone.

I lost a diamond from my wedding ring today, so I took the ring off and put it in my jewelry box until I can decide what I want to do about having it fixed. It seems so strange to me that there is any decision to make, but there really is. In all the massive changes of being widowed, I have begun to look at that ring as the source of my identity. I have clung to it and to what it represents—which is a husband and relationship I no longer have.

Although as a widow, I can continue to carry my husband's name as mine, and I want to do that, I find that people are constantly trying to disassociate me from him. I receive envelopes with "Ms." instead of "Mrs." And if "Mrs." is used, my first name is there instead of his. I don't like it. Even though he's gone, he continues to be my husband in my heart. I don't know why no one understands that and why everyone is in such a hurry to change who I am. That being said, it makes me wonder if I'm clinging too tightly to the past and if that ring is part of the binding. So, while I decide what to do, it will sit in my jewelry box. It is now one more major decision in the process of healing I don't want to make.

I made the four-hour trip to your grave today just to see how you're doing. Doesn't that sound stupid? But the reality is, it's not about how you're doing, but about how I'm doing.

I brought a blanket and spread it on the ground; I began to talk to you and tell you about how I'm doing, what my life is like without you, about the really rough things I'm having trouble coping with, and, so as not to depress you too much, some of the few upbeat things I can remember. I spent some time reading to you a few of my favorite passages from the Bible and sharing what God is doing in my life. Then, as usual, I asked you how things were going in heaven and what it was like. I know it's a silly thing to do, but somehow it makes me feel better.

After I've been with you for a while, the thought comes to me that I have to think about leaving you to return home. Even though I know it's just your body in that grave and that you're actually in heaven now, the sadness of leaving glues me to that blanket on the ground. It always takes me a long time to find the strength to stand up, gather the blanket, and turn toward the car. I find the goodbyes I say now are often as hard as the one I said on the day you were buried. I have yet to leave without a profound sense of loss and tears, but it's okay. It will get better.

Last spring you bought some tomato plants at a roadside stand. I must say, they were pretty pitiful-looking, I laughed at them, and you said not to judge them too critically because they would be like the ugly duckling and do just fine. You were right, and those pitiful plants became massive; they were more than six feet tall, with more tomatoes than I would have ever dreamed. It was a warm summer and fall and tomatoes kept coming, until one day I picked the last one then shortly after that, you died. I wonder if the plants knew they would be the last ones you would see, so they gave it their all just for you?

Today, one spring later, I walked into the yard and was looking at the spot where the tomatoes had been last year, when I looked down and saw them. There, in the warm dirt of spring, were little tomato plants smiling at me. I didn't know whether to laugh or cry, so I did both.

Today was one of those perfect spring days when the sun was brilliant, the breeze was warm and gentle, the scent of spring was in the air, and there was absolutely nothing to do but to enjoy it. I contemplated what to do on this day—and decided to do nothing. So I grabbed a new book I'd been wanting to read, went out on the porch, propped my bare feet up on the railing and started reading.

I don't think I got much past the first couple of pages when I started thinking about you, and how we would have spent the day, and what we would have done. Although there was an ache in my heart, it didn't overwhelm me; I fought the tears and won, and I realized that although you're not here, I can still enjoy spring. I also realized that I was perfectly content on the porch, alone but not lonely; that part was done. It's funny how I never saw loneliness leave, or even realized it was going, but today I realized that the shackles of loneliness were gone and that a newfound freedom replaced it. I will survive.

I am sitting at the kitchen table with my breakfast before me and my eyes wander to "your" place. Often this happens, but today is different. Today, I know it's time. Today, I know I must let you go, and I feel I'm ready. Today, I reach my hand to where yours would be and wrap my fingers around the hand that isn't there. I give it a small squeeze, look into the eyes I dream about, and tell you I love you but it's time. Today, I have to start living again, and to do that I must focus on the present and future and not the past. You, my love, are the past and although you will always be in my heart, you must now take a backseat to my todays. This is a bittersweet day but a necessary one. Thank you for our years together. Thank you for all the good times, and not-so-good times. Thank you for loving me. Thank you for it all. I love you.

⁓ ⚬⸙ ⸙⚬ ⁓

I'm healing, and what do I say about healing except it is a roller coaster of emotions that keeps me reeling as I slowly come to grips with my grief. One day I get up with a positive view of the day and of life, and all is well; then, some little something stabs my heart and I'm crying again. Or, I might go for days without crying, then have two or three days of tears. The good thing about healing is that once I started, I knew that I was on my way to the end of my grief and that, although it's slow, I can now see progress.

Healing is a time of looking at where I've been, where I am, and where I'm going, as I am now beginning to see the light at the end of the tunnel. With this healing, I'm beginning to slowly deal with the things that I haven't been able to look at since my husband's death. I spend a day here and there going through things, remembering and crying. Powerful emotions of grief might overwhelm me again but it's okay, because I'm moving on and this is just a part of it.

I'm finding that healing is a time of renewed emotional strength. I find that I am relishing the ability to smile. Laughter is awesome too, and I'm beginning to do it without guilt. As I heal, I've realized that loneliness has disappeared and that I can now deal with the concept of being alone. I'm reaching out more to others, and the social life I had shunned is something I am slowly beginning to embrace. It is also at this time that it's really becoming clear to me how difficult it is for a widow to have a social life, as the world is paired and I no longer am.

The women I have always been friends with are still here, but I realize that it's different between us; my time is my own, but their time continues to revolve around husbands and coupled obligations I no longer share. This is one of the saddest parts of being a widow; now that I have all this free time, it's hard to find someone to fill it.

Healing is a time of growth, and with it comes growing pains, but it is now that most of my burden of intense grief is falling away. It is now that I know for certain that I will survive. It is also at this time that I am able to look back on all that has happened and see God's hand at work, from the first moment to now. The revelation of His grace and love that has carried me through is so encompassing that the name Savior takes on a whole new meaning.

I'm stumbling over the "grief" questions—all the why, what, and how questions that make me battle so many emotions about life and death. I don't understand why you took him, Lord, and it makes me angry that I have to go on without him. Did I do something wrong so I'm getting punished? Did he do something so wrong that you just couldn't leave him here any longer, and if so, what? Why can't I have answers, and why won't you tell me? The strange thing is, I'm not angry with you, just my inability to understand. However, my place isn't to understand but accept the fact that you are God and have your reasons for what you do. But I still wish I could understand.

I'm moving on with my grieving. I find that I rarely have tears in the morning, although at some point in time during the day they will probably come; but it's okay, because I handle them better than I used to. Sometimes I can even keep them at bay long enough to watch them totally disappear, and sometimes they don't come back at all that day. I don't know when this started but I'm glad I've gotten here, so that I can continue to see some progress throughout this process of grief. With a slowing of tears there is also a sense of humor returning, which has been absent since the start of all this and which I've missed greatly. I have always loved to laugh. At first, I felt guilty about laughing with you dead—as if I was never supposed to laugh again. But one day it struck me that if I had died, I would have wanted you to laugh again and to do it every day; knowing you so well, I know you would feel the same, so I'm now laughing without guilt. I don't know much about this part of my healing, but I do know it feels better.

It dawned on me today that I haven't cried in several days, and that I have handled some problems without feeling entirely overwhelmed. Could it be I'm coming back? I kind of feel like the phoenix rising from the ashes, and it feels good. It really feels good to see "me" again. Not a strong "me" yet, but "me" nonetheless.

Today is one of those days when I'm just numb. I can't bring up an emotion of any kind, and it's the strangest feeling to not have any feeling. I'm not happy, not sad, not content but not discontent, not irritated, angry, frustrated, or anything. I just am. Strange.

However, it's not the first time I've felt this way, and I find that at some time, something will eventually happen to elicit a response from me. So I've learned to go with it and to let it run its course. I find that when I have these times of numbness, it's usually because I'm in some sort of transition emotionally; therefore, I've begun to view all these different emotional states, or lack of them, as times of healing.

I went to buy groceries today and you'd think, after doing it on my own for so long, I would remember to take the bags the checker just filled off the carousel and put them into the cart. But that was your job, and I still can't remember to do it until all the bags are full, the checker has to stop and load them into the cart, and I have to apologize one more time for forgetting to do so myself. Why can't I remember to do this? Maybe I just don't want to.

The weatherman says that thunderstorms are on the way with the possibility of tornadoes and, having lived through a couple of them as a child, I'm fearful. I remember how you would be sitting in your chair calmly watching TV, while I would be frantically putting valuables in the bathroom in the center of the house, which we always used for a "safe" room. Every now and then you'd call me out on the porch, put your arm around my shoulder to view with you, and show me what to look for that would signal danger or safety. I would listen, but not too closely, because you were there, and I knew you would keep me safe. However, tonight is different, as my safety net is gone. I pray the lessons aren't.

⌒ ⌒ᶜ ⌒ꜟ⌒

It's tax time again and I am, as usual, overwhelmed with it. This was one of your areas of expertise, as you had a tax office for many years. You understood all these foreign forms and what they said and what they were for and how to maneuver in the ridiculous maze of a governmental agency out of control. I, on the other hand, am at a loss and, even with the help of a CPA, I have no idea whether any of these forms are right when I sign them.

I've always hated math and anything to do with numbers. Just balancing the checkbook drove me crazy, especially when I was two cents off and couldn't figure out where they had gone. You would always get so frustrated with me because it was so easy for you; you never understood why I had to use the decimal point with a calculator to know where the cents were, but it had to be there. I think after a few years, you finally gave up on the decimal point, accepted my inability to see something that wasn't there, and began to humor me to get through whatever we were working on.

Anyway, here I am again, faced with something I am so totally inept at and having to tackle it without you while doing it, all through tear-filled eyes. Impossible.

⌒ ⌒ᶜ ⌒ꜟ⌒

I was talking to my friend Sue today. She said that her husband
Mike had commented that I had sounded better the other day
when I was talking to him on the phone. Funny, I don't feel bet-
ter, but I'll probably be the last to know because I have trouble
seeing the changes that I know are going on. Although, I was
thinking about me the other day, and I was astounded by things
that I do see have in fact changed. All the things that used to
be important aren't, and all the things that weren't are. Maybe
that's a good thing, in some ways. I do know that I laughed a
few days ago and that it felt good, but I must also admit that I
still felt a little guilty about it, for some reason.

This widow thing is so hard—and if it's hard for me, I have
to wonder what it's like for those who don't have Jesus. How do
they get from day to day? I know that He promised to be with
me, and believe me He has been; He's the only reason I've got-
ten this far. I know that when it gets too rough I can go to Him
in prayer, and that when I cry out I'm comforted. What an awe-
some bit of knowledge to know that when I'm at my weakest I
don't have to worry, because I'm not holding on to Him; He's
holding onto me.

Healing is a strange thing. I went so long carrying the gigantic
burden of grief that threatened to drown me. And then one day,
I woke up, and I noticed there was a subtle difference in the way
the day looked. The next day was better too, so I thought I was
finally moving on and . . . wham. The next minute, the tears
were pouring again and I felt like I was back to square one.

How strange my emotions are and how they play with me
like a cat with a mouse—letting me go, then pouncing, then

letting me go again. Why do they do that? Why can't they just move on in progression without all the stumbling over things I've already been through? Why does it all have to be so hard?

I know I'm going to make it, and I see me getting stronger day by day, but there are still days that seem so much like the days in the very beginning. There are still times when a tiny thing will trigger precious memories, then tears, and I wonder how long this will go on. Maybe it's best that I don't know.

Pictures, tangible memories of life. Tiny snippets of time caught forever in little squares. I'm sitting here today going through all the snippets I can find of our life together, and tears and laughter are vying for first place in my heart. Some of them I can hardly bear to look at and others I can hardly stand to put down. My heart doesn't know what to do with all these memories of time past, and I think it's because it knows there can never be any more memories added. What a sad thought.

I miss you. I miss your sleepy smile and sweet kiss first thing in the morning, the smell of your coffee, sitting on the bathroom counter watching you shave, and the smell of your cologne. I miss you looking over my shoulder as I cook, and the way you would always peel the onions because for some reason they didn't make you cry. I miss the feel of your arm around my shoulder and your kiss on the back of my neck—and, when you wanted to make a point, the way you would put your hands on my shoulders and look down into my eyes and say what was on your mind. I miss coming to you and having you wrap your arms around me and laying my head against your chest, and the feeling that nothing in the world could touch me as long as I stayed in the circle of those arms. I miss the feel of you next to me in bed as we would cuddle together to go to sleep. I miss your touch, the scent of you, the sight of you, the warmth of you, and the sound of that deep, resonant voice that quelled my fears, drove my passions, and fed my heart with love. I simply miss you.

⁓ ୧ ⁓

For the longest time, the sight of couples made me cry. I had such a difficult time watching as they would touch each other in the little ways that couples do. She would lay her hand on his arm to get his attention to show him something, or he would put his hand on the small of her back to guide her through a door—little things they didn't even think about, but which make up the language of couples. He, leaning down to whisper something in her ear, and the tilt of her head as she looked up at him and smiled, or the way their hands found each other as they walked along.

But now, I'm able to watch without tears and often smile at these couples, because I remember what it was like to be one of them. Do I miss it? Yes, but I miss it with the one I had—and right now, the thought of another in that place is something I can't comprehend—so I smile and walk on.

⁓ ୧ ⁓

I lie awake and watch the shadows on the wall, silken fingers of the night that silently glide across a blank stage, and then are gone until the next car passes or the cat walks in front of the nightlight, and my mind silently glides across a blank stage of its own as memories come and go much as the shadows. No tears, no heartache, no grieving, just memories of a life that no longer exists but a love that lives on. I find I am coming to this place more and more often because where once it brought tears, it now brings comfort, as I remember you and me and us. I also find that leaving this place to go back to the real world is easier, because I can carry you in my heart now without you interfering with my moving on. Not that you are forgotten, but I am more comfortable with my feelings, and my grief is giving way to an acceptance of life without you— and isn't that what grieving is? A long, hard road to acceptance.

Do you know what else I've been doing lately? I've been laughing and laughing at things no one else seems to see the humor in, and at stupid things I wouldn't begin to try to share, and it's wonderful! Oh, how I've missed laughing. I've always found humor in little things and it's so fun to be able to see those silly little things again and respond. How great it feels to heal, and that's what I'm doing in increasingly bigger ways that are constantly reassuring me that the end is near—not the end of my remembrance of you, but the end of my inability to get back to living again and on focusing on someone besides myself. This is so good!

Someone asked me the strangest question the other day. She said, "Are you dating?"

Dating. It's definitely been long enough since you died and yes, I've thought about it. But each time I did, it made my stomach churn and my heart stumble for a second, and then I felt an intense feeling of guilt that I was cheating on you by even thinking about it.

No, I'm not dating, and at this point I doubt I ever do. I've gotten past the unbearable loneliness that sends so many into the dating arena much too soon and am now content going from day to day taking care of myself and my responsibilities. I'm not ready for dating, I may never be ready for dating—and that, in itself, is okay.

I've noticed a change in my mindset recently, and what I'm seeing is a good thing. For the first time, I'm really looking at others again and seeing that I'm not the only one who is hurting, and my heart is starting to respond to their pain. I'm beginning to want to be the comforter instead of the comforted and, with this change, I'm finding an inner peace I haven't felt in a long while. I'm looking at the world in a more positive light and wanting to become part of it again.

I am alone now—not lonely, just alone—and there is such a major difference between the two. Loneliness was a monster that was always on the verge of devouring me, while alone is simply that—alone. Alone is okay, and I'm finding that there are both good things and not-so-good things about being alone, as there are with most situations.

The major problem with being alone is the adjustment of doing so much by myself, of not having a backup person to ask for advice on things I know so little about, or of not having anyone around to ask to lend an extra pair of hands while doing household chores. How am I going to move the eighty-pound bag of potting soil I never would have bought in the first place? How do I get used to eating alone in a restaurant, or not being able to share the evening's magnificent sunset with someone else? Traveling isn't so much fun either because there isn't anyone to share the experience with. And the list goes on and on.

On the other hand, if I want to carpet the walls, paint the floor, and panel the ceiling, there is no one to complain about it. I can cook and eat what I want, when I want; and if I want to make a pot of soup and eat it three times a day for three days that's okay, too. I can make plans without having to worry if anyone else will be inconvenienced, and I can go and stay as long as I want. Being alone gives me a freedom I haven't had in years and, although I wouldn't have chosen this, I am now at a point where I am able to look at it differently than I could even six months ago. I can now acknowledge the fact that I am alone without the pain and dread that used to be associated with it. I'm buoyed by the knowledge that I am healing, and I am going to be all right.

After the loneliness goes, the acceptance of being alone is a slow process, kind of like easing into the water at the beginning of summer. First you dip in the toes of one foot, then the whole foot, then you add the other, and progress until you're finally out there swimming around—and so it goes with alone.

Fall is coming, and although the leaves are still green they're beginning to take on the brittle look of approaching death. I sit here alone in the woods and listen to the snapping and cracking as pine cones, small limbs, and twigs tumble down. Even the leaves that most think of as silently falling make a staccato sound of their own on their wind-blown flutter to the ground.

The insects humming and droning by seem to be telling me the season is about to change. I must hurry to enjoy it, as the warm days of fall are about to be replaced with sweaters, and then the heavy coats of winter. I love this transition from summer to fall. I love the change of color and the seasonal flavor of apple cider, and pumpkin bread and pie, and the smell of burning leaves.

I feel sad for people who never experience seasons. What wonders and memories they miss as the spring brings forth a new generation that matures through summer, ages in fall, and dies in winter, only to be reborn again in spring. It only takes one year of seasons to understand a lifetime of living. I'm in my fall now and will soon be approaching the winter of my life, but I look forward to that, too. However, right now, I hear turkeys in the distance, the deer quietly easing through the foliage, and I have a fall to enjoy.

I spent the evening with friends and, although I was the only single person in the group, it was okay. The sadness that used to overwhelm me in being the only one without a partner has gone, and I'm enjoying the company of others without thinking about it. That is an unbelievable amount of progress since the beginning of all this, and I'm really reveling in my growth. I'm now able to embrace new things, most of the time, without feeling as if half of me is missing—and it's wonderful.

I have been through the darkest of nights
Been through the valley of death
Walked with the ache of a heart
That struggled to ever find rest

I have waded through oceans of tears
Trudged on through the thick muck of grief
Struggled to hold up my head
As I searched for a semblance of peace

I have wallowed in gloom and despair
Tottered on the edge of the pit
Fought to gain some control
Of pieces that no longer fit

I have gone on my face to the floor
Cried out for the mercy of God
Brazenly throwing my pain
At the feet of my Jesus I love

I have prayed for the strength to go on
Begged for heartache to cease
Pleaded for even a glimpse
Of some sort of hurried release

I have asked from the depth of my heart
For the things that I thought I'd need
Then the quiet voice of my Lord
Said be still and let me lead

I have the peace you are seeking
I'll carry you through it all

I'll never leave or forsake you
I'll never let you fall

I have accepted the promise given
I've watched Him unfold His plan
Been amazed at the healing accomplished
Through my Jesus the great I AM

Questions for Grievers

Take some time now to think through, process, and write down your responses to each of the questions below. Use the additional space provided below to record your answers.

1. What baby steps, and what stops and starts, have you experienced during your own grieving process? How have you recognized aspects of healing, even in the midst of that process?

_____

_____

_____

_____

_____

_____

_____

_____

_____

_____

_____

_____

_____

_____

_____

_____

_____

_____

_____

_____

_____

_____

2. Are you laughing yet? If so, how does that make you feel? If
   not, why not?

_____

_____

_____

_____

_____

_____

_____

_____

_____

_____

_____

_____

_____

_____

_____

_____

_____

_____

_____

_____

_____

_____

_____

_____

_____

3. Do you find it frightening to let go of the past and move forward? If so, why? If not, why not?

_____

_____

_____

_____

_____

_____

_____

_____

_____

_____

_____

_____

_____

_____

_____

_____

_____

_____

_____

_____

_____

_____

_____

_____

_____

_____

_____

4. Jesus commanded us to forgive, but it isn't always easy to do. Do you have something to forgive your spouse for that you're struggling with? Do you have anything you need to forgive yourself for? Are you ready to forgive? If not, why not?

_____

_____

_____

_____

_____

_____

_____

_____

_____

_____

_____

_____

_____

_____

_____

_____

_____

_____

_____

_____

_____

_____

_____

_____

5. How have you begun to experience acceptance of your alone-
   ness, where once it felt only like loss?

_____

_____

_____

_____

_____

_____

_____

_____

_____

_____

_____

_____

_____

_____

_____

_____

_____

_____

_____

_____

_____

_____

_____

_____

_____

The Other Side of Grief

There is an old saying, "You never know how much you need Jesus until Jesus is all you have," and it's so true. From the first time I met my Savior, I knew I loved Him—but I never knew how much I needed Him until He was all I had. When I came home and found my husband dead in his chair, I remember my first word was, "*No!*" And after he was taken away, I remember sitting on the floor and, through the numbness, my next word was, "*Why?*" and then, "*How?*" *Why did you take him, and how will I go on?*

I'm still amazed that I made it through that first day and through all the events that followed. Looking back, they're so vivid, and yet they were a blur of activity. I do remember one thing very, very clearly—I remember that my first prayer was short and sweet: "Please dear God, get me through this." Seven little words that changed everything.

I know it was then that He picked me up, and when I had nothing, He became all I had and all I needed. I have relied on Him time after time after time, and never has He let me down. I have learned to pray in ways I never would have, had I not had to go through this, and I have come to know with absolute rock-ribbed assurance that my Jesus is all I need—and, more to the point, all I have, as everything here is temporary. I look at life differently now. I know what it is to have nothing, and yet, have everything.

After all this time, after all the agony of grief, after my inability to grasp the "whys" of it all, after all the darkness, after all the myriad of emotions, after everything, I realize through it all, there was you, Lord. It isn't that I ever thought you weren't with me, because you have been my strength the whole time, but it has just really dawned on me what and who you are.

You . . . are . . . *God!* You are the magnificent Creator of the universe, the one who spoke everything into existence, and yet, you . . . know . . . me. I am overwhelmed today with this understanding. Every time I went on my face before you in the depths of my despair you knew it. Every time I called out to you, I was heard; every time I struggled through tears and questions and the aching of my heart, you were my comforter, my caregiver, my companion, my strength, my all.

Today, I realize that I will never understand why you do what you do. Today, I understand that it isn't my place to know and that's OK. One of the Bible verses that was quoted to me so many times in the beginning was Romans 8:28—"all things work together for good"—and at the time people were reminding me of this my thought was, "Who cares?" Because at the time, that was the last thing I wanted to hear. I couldn't see what good might come out of losing the love of my life and that verse became, to me, something people said because they had nothing else to say. It was meaningless.

But now, I read Romans 8:28 and my heart understands. Now, after all this time, I can look back and see the good things. I can look back and see how my leaning on you has built my faith. I can see the Cornerstone in perspective and am humbled. I can remember how my ability to pray grew from simple to complex prayers that were the spilling over of a heart that was learning to love as never before. Now, I . . . know . . . you. I may not understand what you do or why you do it but, I don't care, and I don't care because now I trust in a way I never have before. Through this grief of mine, you have become so real that my heart swells to bursting with the joy of it.

I am saddened by the thought of those who become angry with you for their loss. It's as if they never realized there is such a thing as death and then need someone to blame, so they blame you. Granted, from a human perspective, your timing can be devastating. Why take a child of any age, or a young parent, and why so many ways that are heartbreaking? Could you have changed the ending of these lives? Yes. Could you have healed everyone and fixed all the broken body pieces? Yes. Could you make it all perfect? Yes. But, you don't. And you don't because we don't live in the Garden of Eden anymore. We live in a fallen world where people make up the god they want and then are furious when their god doesn't come through for them as they think he should. Even those who think of themselves as strong Christians sometimes stumble over the death of a loved one. Why? Christians aren't promised to miss the complexities of life.

I love the name you gave yourself in Exodus 3:14, "I Am That I Am," and so you are. How pregnant that is with meanings that birth themselves, as I keep coming to more and more knowledge of who you are and what you have done and continue to do in my life.

I am at the end of my grieving now. I find I can think of you without tears or heartache, for those things have been replaced with sweet memories. I can talk about you without tears yet, sometimes the memories are so sweet that the tears still come, but they aren't tears of grief any more, but of fond remembrance. You are still as much a part of me as ever, and I find myself talking to you every now and then when I need another viewpoint because you were always so wise.

I still miss you, and I always will. I don't find anything unhealthy about this, as I'm moving on with my life and growing stronger daily. My thoughts and actions are no longer wrapped around your death and my loss. Still, you still pop up from time to time—and that's okay.

I keep pictures of us around me and I like looking at them, but that seems like forever ago, and I'm making new memories with new friends and activities. I have done a lot of growing through this experience and learned a lot about myself. I like this new me who is stronger and wiser and more capable of handling whatever life has to offer. But most of all, I love the firsthand knowledge of what it's like to know and understand the last line of that "Footprints" poem: "It was then that I carried you." With the quiet strength of my precious Jesus, I have survived the journey to the other side of grief.

Questions for Grievers

Take some time now to think through, process, and write down your responses to each of the questions below. Use the additional space provided below to record your answers.

1. What does the end of grieving look like to you?

_____

_____

_____

_____

_____

_____

_____

_____

_____

_____

_____

_____

_____

_____

_____

_____

_____

_____

_____

_____

_____

_____

_____

_____

2. What do you want for your new life? What are your plans
   to achieve it?

_____

_____

_____

_____

_____

_____

_____

_____

_____

_____

_____

_____

_____

_____

_____

_____

_____

_____

_____

_____

_____

_____

_____

_____